25 TALES OF CREATIVE THINKERS

Good Night Stories for Rebel Girls and Rebel Girls are registered trademarks.
Good Night Stories for Rebel Girls and all other Rebel Girls titles are available for bulk purchase for sale promotions, premiums, fundraising, and educational needs.
For details, write to sales@rebelgirls.com.

This is a work of creative nonfiction. It is a collection of heartwarming and thought-provoking stories inspired by the lives and adventures of 25 influential women. It is not an encyclopedic account of the events and accomplishments of their lives.

www.rebelgirls.com

Some of the artwork in this book has been previously published in the books *Good Night Stories for Rebel Girls 2*, *Good Night Stories for Rebel Girls: 100 Real-Life Tales of Black Girl Magic*, and *Good Night Stories for Rebel Girls: 100 Inspiring Young Changemakers*.

Library of Congress Control Number: 2023942026
Rebel Girls, Inc.
421 Elm Ave.
Larkspur, CA 94939

Text by Shadae Mallory
Art direction by Giulia Flamini
Cover illustrations by Joanne Dertili
Graphic design by Kristen Brittain
Edited by Eliza Kirby
Special thanks: Hannah Bennett, Sarah Parvis, Amy Pfister, Gulnaz Saiyed, Sarah Clark, Ennis Bashe, Guntaas Kaur Chugh, Anna Everts, Amy Bowen

Printed in China, 2023
10 9 8 7 6 5 4 3 2 1
001-340077-Feb'24
ISBN: 979-8-88964-027-1

FSC
www.fsc.org
MIX
Paper | Supporting responsible forestry
FSC™ C018179

CONTENTS

FOREWORD

Dear Rebels,

My name is Isabella Springmühl. I'm 26 years old, I am from Guatemala, and I am a fashion designer. I speak all over the world about entrepreneurship and employment inclusion for people with disabilities. What I love most about myself is that I have Down syndrome.

Down syndrome means my brain works differently than other people's, and it's just one example of neurodiversity. From a young age, I had the opportunity to attend a traditional school, which gave me great confidence, even though connecting with my peers wasn't always easy. My mother took it upon herself to educate and inform my teachers about Down syndrome. She had the brilliant idea of writing a book so that my classmates could also learn about this condition. They learned about me, and in turn, I learned about them. Today, I know that being different made me strive harder, and with the support of a shadow teacher and curriculum adaptations, I graduated college. My classmates even chose me to deliver the graduation speech.

I dreamed of pursuing a degree in fashion design, but I was turned down by two universities in Guatemala. It wasn't because I lacked talent or knowledge. It was because I had Down syndrome. I felt devastated because, for the first time in my life, Down syndrome was a reason to be denied an opportunity.

But I didn't let that stop me. My journey as a fashion designer began with a passion for beautiful clothes and jewelry, which turned into a thriving business, positively impacting the lives of many Guatemalan artists. I developed a unique and self-taught creative process. I make vibrant pieces crafted from pre-loved Guatemalan fabrics. With the help of a wonderful all-girl team, I bring my ideas, creativity, and deep love for my country to life.

The most challenging part of my journey has been dealing with the lack of understanding about my condition. But understanding comes with knowledge. That's why books like this one are so important. Through them, people all over the world can learn what it means to be neurodivergent, and neurodivergent readers can see themselves on the page.

I'm excited for you to read about the incredible neurodivergent women in *Rebel Girls Celebrate Neurodiversity*. Some are autistic, some are dyslexic, some have ADHD—and all have achieved great things. I particularly love Temple Grandin's story. Not only does her life inspire me, but her famous phrase, "Different, not less," echoes constantly in my mind. To me, this means that no matter what we face, we deserve to have the opportunities to grow, develop, and be included in our society. Similarly, the remarkable story of Madeline Stuart, who shattered beauty stereotypes and demonstrated that fashion is for everyone, really resonates with me.

These are just a couple of the inspiring neurodivergent women you'll meet in this book. These Rebels show that resilience and creativity are the most important ingredients when you're following your dreams. With love, imagination, hard work, and most of all, embracing your uniqueness, you can turn your dreams into reality.

—Isabella Springmühl

SCAN TO HEAR MORE!

BONUS! AUDIO STORIES!

Download the Rebel Girls app to hear longer stories about some of the impactful creators and leaders in this book and discover tales of other trailblazing women. Whenever you come across a gear icon, scan the code, and you'll be whisked away on an audio adventure. Scan this code to learn more about Isabella!

AMANDA GORMAN

POET

SCAN TO HEAR MORE!

One cold January morning, Amanda Gorman approached a podium, took a deep breath, and began to speak. Millions of people from around the world watched as she recited her poem "The Hill We Climb." It was the 2021 inauguration of President Joe Biden, and she was the youngest inaugural poet in US history! When she was finished, the crowd cheered for her beautiful words and moving performance. Amanda was proud of herself. She knew there was a time in her life when saying a poem aloud would not have been so easy. When she was a little girl, Amanda was diagnosed with an auditory processing disorder.

People with auditory processing disorders can hear, but their brains have a hard time making sense of sounds. This can make it difficult to have conversations, follow directions, or learn new words. For Amanda this was especially true when she tried to say certain words and sounds, like *r* and *sh* sounds. Writing, however—that didn't pose those same challenges. From a young age she found solace writing poems. She worked hard to create a voice and style that was entirely her own. Before long, she had enough to fill a book. She called it *The One for Whom Food Is Not Enough*.

Writing poems was one thing, reciting them was another. As Amanda got ready for the inauguration, she focused on her inner voice. She knew what she had to say was powerful, and she could spread her message of hope and togetherness. She practiced by reading aloud. It helped her develop a strong voice and the courage to perform in front of others. The letter *r* still gave her trouble—especially when she had to say the word *rise* many lines in a row—but that didn't matter. Amanda led with her strengths, and the world heard what she had to say.

BORN MARCH 7, 1998
UNITED STATES OF AMERICA

"I DON'T CONSIDER HAVING A SPEECH IMPEDIMENT NECESSARILY AS A DISABILITY BUT ACTUALLY AS A STRENGTH. IT GAVE ME MY GREATEST SUPERPOWER, WHICH IS MY VOICE."
—AMANDA GORMAN

ILLUSTRATION BY KETURAH ARIEL

BILLIE EILISH

SINGER-SONGWRITER

SCAN TO HEAR MORE!

When Billie was little, she and her brother spent their free time writing songs together. She loved finding the perfect words to match the melody and hearing the way her voice moved through them all, from soft whispers to airy high notes. She always knew she wanted to be a singer. When she was 13, Billie uploaded her song "Ocean Eyes" on a streaming platform. Listeners loved it, and the world wanted to see what Billie would do next! Out of the spotlight, though, Billie was dealing with a neurological condition.

When she was 11 years old, Billie noticed her body moving on its own. She would raise her eyebrows, wiggle her ears back and forth, click her jaw, or flex her muscles—all without being able to control it. Billie did not know why this was happening to her. With help from her family and doctors, she found out that she had Tourette's syndrome, a condition that affected the nerves in her body. It caused her tics—the sudden movements that kept happening throughout the day. Billie was relieved to know what was going on, but she still had a hard time with the tics, like when people would laugh at her. That made her upset.

Over time, Billie embraced Tourette's syndrome. "It's not like I like it," she says, "but I feel like it's . . . part of me." Some of her tics have gone away as she's gotten older. She still experiences others. Through it all, she's focused on what really matters—her music! Billie uses lots of different sounds, from electronic beats and catchy bass lines to soft guitar chords and plinking piano notes. Above it all, her gentle, expressive voice intones heartfelt lyrics.

Billie keeps speaking out about her experience with Tourette's syndrome. She wants everyone to feel comfortable sharing what they're going through.

BORN DECEMBER 18, 2001
UNITED STATES OF AMERICA

"WRITING A SONG IS SO PERSONAL. YOU HAVE TO HAVE TRUST IN SOMEONE YOU'RE WORKING WITH; OTHERWISE, YOU'RE NOT GONNA COME OUT WITH SOMETHING THAT'S REALLY YOU."
—BILLIE EILISH

ILLUSTRATION BY PAULA ZORITE

BREANNA CLARK

RUNNER

Powerful strides carried a young woman swiftly around the racetrack. Behind her, seven other women raced for their chance at a Paralympic gold medal. The stands were filled with thousands of people, excited to see who would win. As their cheers grew louder and louder, Breanna Clark crossed the finish line. Her heart raced. She couldn't believe it—she had won!

As a little girl, Breanna was incredibly active and curious. She enjoyed playing sports, making friends, and spending time with her twin brother, Rashard. When she was four, Breanna's parents noticed that she was not like other children. They took her to the doctor and found out that she was autistic. Autism often affects how people talk, act, and think.

Breanna's parents were worried about her and her future. But they didn't need to be concerned. Breanna always knew what she loved—being active! She tried several sports, but none of them were as fun as running. In high school, Breanna joined the track and field team. That meant she got to run as much as she wanted. She even started competing in races.

In 2016, Breanna qualified for the Paralympics, an international competition for athletes with disabilities. She won gold! Five years later, her powerful legs and incredible focus took her across the finish line at the Tokyo Paralympics. She picked up a gold medal there, too.

Breanna's victories make her and her family proud. She keeps blowing past the competition all over the world.

BORN NOVEMBER 4, 1994

UNITED STATES OF AMERICA

"I LIKE RUNNING BECAUSE
IT MAKES ME FEEL FREE."
—BREANNA CLARK

ILLUSTRATION BY
CARLA JAYE

CAMILLA PANG

SCIENTIST AND AUTHOR

Once upon a time, there was a girl named Camilla who always wanted to know how things worked. She would watch *The Lion King* and play the songs on her xylophone, tapping out the tunes until she understood the patterns in the music. When Camilla was eight, she was diagnosed with autism. That made her want to learn even more. She spent hours and hours reading science books and trying to understand how humans work. *If I learn about humans as a group*, she thought, *maybe I can better understand myself.*

Camilla's family was always behind her. Her dad is an engineer and showed her the splendor of science. Her mom is an artist and showed her the beauty in the world. They both made Camilla feel brave so she could learn lots of things and share them with other people.

As Camilla got older, she kept learning. She wrote lots of notes in more than 60 notebooks! She used her own experiences to figure out how people act and talk to each other. She also used stories from her life to make a guide to understanding people's behavior.

She put everything she had learned into a book called *Explaining Humans* so others could read about her experiences with being neurodivergent. Her book was released worldwide, and soon people began inviting her to give talks and lectures. As Camilla went on tour to share her stories, she showed everyone what people with disabilities can accomplish. She continues to write beautiful books to help people understand neurodiversity and celebrate her love for science.

BORN FEBRUARY 1992

UNITED KINGDOM

"I KNOW THAT [WRITING] WILL ANCHOR ME IN FEELING HUMAN FOR THE REST OF MY LIFE."
—CAMILLA PANG

ILLUSTRATION BY
VERONICA GUARINO

CHAMIQUE HOLDSCLAW

BASKETBALL PLAYER

The basketball net swooshed. Another successful basket made by Chamique Holdsclaw! Fans cheered from the stands. The buzzer sounded, signaling the end of the game. The team celebrated their win as they left the court. It should have been an exciting moment, but Chamique found it difficult to focus on the happiness of the victory.

Chamique always loved basketball, and she had always been good at the game. Her rise to fame began when she joined the University of Tennessee basketball team. *Swoosh! Swoosh! Swoosh!* Game after game, basket after basket, Chamique dominated on the court. Soon she was the team's top scorer.

Basketball was easy for Chamique. Managing her feelings was harder. Her emotions had been intense for as long as she could remember, and it only became more noticeable as she grew up. When she was happy, she felt incredibly happy, and when she was sad, she felt overwhelmingly sad. At the time, Chamique didn't know how to express what she was going through.

It wasn't until she was older that she found out she had bipolar disorder. Bipolar disorder is a mental health condition that makes it difficult for people to manage their emotions. It can make them feel happy, sad, or angry in a moment. For Chamique, the diagnosis made sense.

Now Chamique wanted to help people understand mental health. She wrote a book called *Breaking Through: Beating the Odds Shot after Shot* about her basketball career and her experiences with bipolar disorder. She wants to make sure that people don't feel ashamed of having mental health issues.

Chamique has made a big difference—on and off the court.

BORN AUGUST 9, 1977
UNITED STATES OF AMERICA

"IT'S NOTHING SPECIAL. I JUST KNOW A LOT OF PEOPLE SUFFER IN SILENCE, AND I'VE GOT TO STEP UP. I'VE GOT TO STAND FOR SOMETHING AND TAKE RESPONSIBILITY."
—CHAMIQUE HOLDSCLAW

ILLUSTRATION BY KATIE CRUMPTON

DARIA SAVILLE

TENNIS PLAYER

Standing on the tennis court, Daria took a deep breath and tried to concentrate on the ball. Her attention deficit hyperactivity disorder (ADHD) made it hard for her to ignore the busy environment of the tournament around her. She could hear the *THWACK* of the tennis ball from a match happening nearby. Spectators cheered, players came on and off the courts, and umpires made calls for other matches even as Daria's continued. She could hardly focus long enough to see the ball hurtling toward her. It was too late. The ball sailed past her. With a deep sigh, Daria accepted her defeat.

Daria knew she was a great tennis player. She had won countless matches and made her way to the Women's Tennis Association's Top 100, a special list of the best players in the entire league. After recovering from an injury, she kept playing until she'd climbed more than a thousand spots in the rankings, earning the title of WTA Comeback Player of the Year. Even competing in a Grand Slam tournament like this one—one of the most important events a tennis player can play in—was a huge accomplishment. But as she walked off the court, she felt angry and disappointed.

After her experience at the tournament, Daria spoke out about what it's like to compete as an athlete with ADHD. Her fans loved her honesty when she wrote about how hard it could be to play at these big outdoor events. They also love that she always comes back to the court. No matter the outcome of a match, Daria keeps playing and speaking up, showing the power of her strength, resilience, and determination.

BORN MARCH 5, 1994
AUSTRALIA AND RUSSIA

"TAKING IT DAY BY DAY, CELEBRATING THE SMALL WINS AND HAVING SMALL GOALS IS THE KEY TO STAYING MOTIVATED."
—DARIA SAVILLE

ESMÉ WEIJUN WANG

AUTHOR

SCAN TO HEAR MORE!

Once upon a time in Michigan, there was an imaginative little girl named Esmé. She was always writing. Her pencil scratched against the page as she filled notebooks with poems. Once, she randomly chose an Olympic athlete from the encyclopedia and wrote a whole essay about them. In fifth grade, she spun the tale of a girl who had been turned into a cat—and it was almost 300 pages long! She enjoyed storytelling so much that she went to college to learn more about writing. But as Esmé got older, she could feel something unusual happening in her brain. There was a daunting feeling of fogginess forming in her mind, and she couldn't figure out what it was.

Soon, Esmé began to have hallucinations, seeing and hearing things that weren't really there. As she worked with doctors to figure out what she was experiencing, she continued writing. She wrote about her hallucinations, her mood swings, and how her everyday experiences made her feel. Her writing grew stronger with every word she wrote.

It took a long time for Esmé to get the right diagnosis. After almost 10 years, she was diagnosed with schizoaffective disorder, which causes people to see and hear things that aren't real. Everything she had experienced finally made sense. That moment marked the start of healing for her journey ahead. "Some people dislike diagnoses, disagreeably calling them boxes and labels," Esmé says. But for Esmé, it's comforting to know that she's not alone, and that other people have been through what she has.

Esmé turned her writing into a book called *The Collected Schizophrenia*s. Her story of living with schizoaffective disorder was open and personal. Esmé understood her own mind better now—and so did readers everywhere.

BORN JUNE 8, 1983
UNITED STATES OF AMERICA

"JUST BECAUSE YOU HAVE
LIMITATIONS . . . DOESN'T
MEAN YOU CAN'T GO ON TO
BUILD RESILIENCE AND A
LEGACY."
—ESMÉ WEIJUN WANG

FAHIMA ABDULRAHMAN

VIDEO JOURNALIST

SCAN TO HEAR MORE!

Fahima hit refresh on her computer. It was almost time for her newest story to post. As a video journalist, she filmed hours of footage, talked to dozens of people, and spent late nights editing everything together to get to this point: a polished video on the BBC News website.

Her eyes lit up when her story appeared.

Fahima grew up far away from the newsroom in England. She was born in Somalia, but she spent her childhood in Syria as a refugee. A refugee is someone who has to leave their home country because it's not safe anymore. Times were difficult for her family, but Fahima loved going to school. However, she had a hard time reading. Whenever teachers asked her to read aloud in class, she mixed up the words. Her teachers thought she just couldn't read. Fahima knew that wasn't true—she could read, just not the way her classmates did.

When she was 16, Fahima's family moved to England. It was hard enough to catch up with her classmates in a new school. But Fahima had to do it in a new language—English. English has a totally different alphabet than Arabic, which she spoke in Syria. After countless hours of studying, Fahima mastered English and got into college.

In college, Fahima loved her film classes. She enjoyed being able to use images to tell stories. As she made friends, Fahima heard other students talking about dyslexia. Dyslexia can make it harder for someone to learn how to read and write. The more she researched dyslexia, the more Fahima's unique brain made sense.

After graduating, Fahima started working for BBC News in London. She wanted to tell real stories of refugees like her. She put a lot of care into getting each video just right. Soon, she was asked to make more and more. Whenever a new video posts, Fahima loves seeing one of her stories out in the world.

BORN AUGUST 22, 1988

SOMALIA, SYRIA, AND UNITED KINGDOM

"I SPEAK THREE LANGUAGES AND MAKE SPELLING AND GRAMMAR MISTAKES IN ALL OF THEM. IT'S JUST PART OF WHO I AM."
—FAHIMA ABDULRAHMAN

ILLUSTRATION BY ELIZABETH MONTERO SANTA

GRETA THUNBERG

CLIMATE ACTIVIST

SCAN TO HEAR MORE!

Once there was a girl who cared deeply about the planet. Greta first learned about climate change when she was eight years old. It made her very worried. The weather was mild where Greta lived in Sweden, but temperatures were getting hotter every year. By the time she was 11, Greta was so scared about climate change that she had stopped eating and talking.

Her parents took her to a doctor. The doctor gave her three diagnoses: autism, obsessive compulsive disorder (OCD), and selective mutism. Her parents were relieved to have answers. Knowing Greta's concern for the environment wouldn't go away, they understood they needed to support her. With their help, Greta turned her fear into activism.

In 2018, Greta made the bold choice to leave her Friday classes to protest outside the Swedish Parliament building. Soon, other people joined in.

Sometimes, Greta's disabilities benefitted her. OCD can give someone a strong focus on certain things. For Greta, it was her work to protect the environment. When people have selective mutism, they do not talk in certain situations or around certain people. Greta says this means, "I only speak when I think it is necessary." The environmental crisis is one of those times.

Greta continues to speak up in front of world leaders. She raises her voice in rooms full of powerful people, demanding change to save the environment. Sometimes she is the youngest person there. But when her words echo through the microphone, people sit up and listen. Greta proves that celebrating people's differences has the power to change the world.

BORN JANUARY 3, 2003

SWEDEN

ILLUSTRATION BY
PAU ZAMRO

"GIVEN THE RIGHT
CIRCUMSTANCES—
BEING DIFFERENT IS
A SUPERPOWER."
—GRETA THUNBERG

JILLIAN GALLAYS

WRESTLER

The wrestling mat felt soft beneath Jillian's feet. She waited for her cue to start the match. Although she was nervous, she reminded herself she didn't get the nickname Jilla Killa for nothing. Competing in the Olympics had always been a dream of Jillian's, and she was thrilled to be representing Team Canada.

When she was young, Jillian looked forward to going to school—not for the classroom but for the wrestling mat. Jillian started wrestling competitively in ninth grade. She enjoyed being on the mat. There, she felt like her true self. The other parts of school, though, weren't as fun for Jillian. Growing up, she had a hard time reading, writing, and spelling. She would mix up letters, write words backward, and even form letters upside down. It made it difficult for Jillian to learn. She didn't know why until a doctor told her she had dyslexia.

In college, Jillian worked toward a degree in kinesiology, the study of human body movement. She did well on the college wrestling team, but she struggled with her courses—they were harder than any classes she'd taken before. But she didn't give up. In order to continue wrestling, Jillian had to keep her grades up. It took seven years to finish her degree, and Jillian graduated in 2012. Then she set out to tackle her next dream: to compete in the Olympic Games.

Jillian trained with all her heart, practicing her pins, escapes, and takedowns. She won the Canadian National Champion title six times before competing in the 2016 Summer Olympics. Jillian did not win a medal, but with her determination and perseverance, she knows that more great things are in store for her.

BORN OCTOBER 20, 1986
CANADA

24

"IT'S IMPORTANT TO PUSH THE BOUNDARIES OF OUR SPORT AND SHOW PEOPLE WHAT WE'RE CAPABLE OF."
—JILLIAN GALLAYS

ILLUSTRATION BY ERICA ROOT

JIYA RAI

Choppy ocean waves glistened as Jiya closed in on the final stretch of the Palk Strait. It had taken her 13 hours and 10 minutes. Now 13-year-old Jiya was about to become the youngest and fastest woman to swim the 18 miles between Sri Lanka and India. Jiya cut through the water, cool droplets streaming from her swim cap. She had come a long way—and not just today.

By age two, Jiya showed signs of autism. She didn't talk, and she wasn't interested in playing with other kids—and her parents didn't know why. When they found out Jiya was autistic, they weren't sure what to think. *Can she still go to school? Can she still find things she loves to do?* they wondered.

Jiya started school, but it was challenging. She was nonverbal, meaning she didn't speak. She could understand what was happening around her, and she had her own way of communicating. Other kids at her school didn't get it. They made fun of Jiya for being different.

But everything changed when the school hosted a swimming competition. Jiya was a natural swimmer. In the water, she was happy and at peace. She competed and won two gold medals. Suddenly everyone in school saw the amazing things Jiya could do.

Competing quickly became Jiya's passion. She swam in meets against other schools and caught the attention of a coach. Having a trainer was the extra push Jiya needed. Soon, she was competing on a national level. Medal after medal, Jiya's confidence blossomed. That was when she started doing open-water swims in the ocean.

Jiya trains every day to be able to swim farther and faster. Nothing can stop her now!

BORN MAY 10, 2008

INDIA

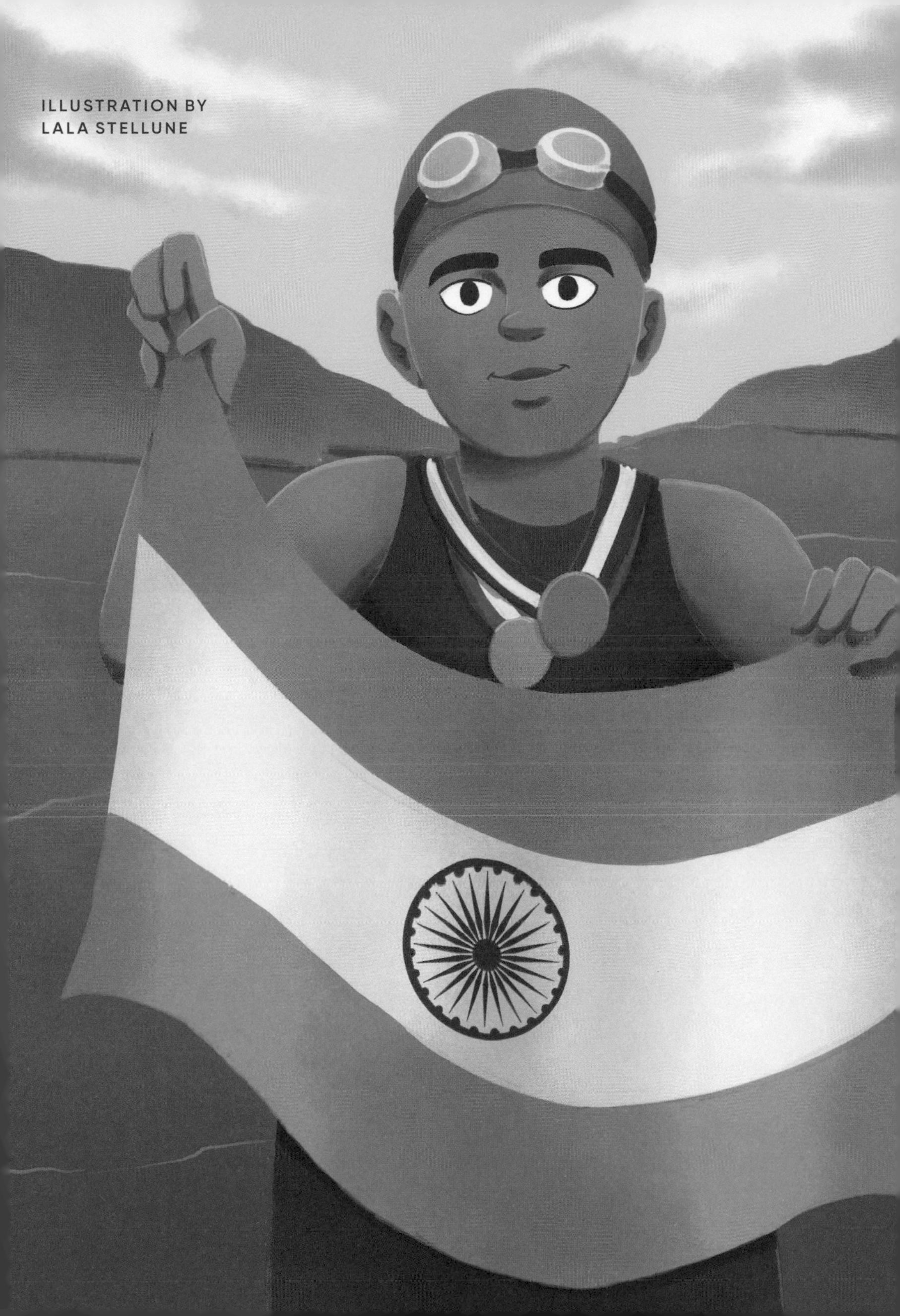

ILLUSTRATION BY
LALA STELLUNE

JULIA BASCOM

ACTIVIST AND EXECUTIVE DIRECTOR

Once upon a time, there was a girl who played differently from other kids. Instead of creating imaginative worlds with dolls, Julia would pace around her backyard. Sometimes she would flap her hands or shake a book while she walked. For hours each day, Julia paced until the grass was worn down and her dad asked her to move to a different part of the yard. The whole time, she recited lists or practiced speeches aloud or in her head.

To the people around her, what Julia was doing didn't look like playing. But Julia was enjoying herself. She was autistic, and she knew these behaviors weren't a problem she needed to fix—they were part of who she was.

When she got older, Julia volunteered as a teacher's aide in special education classrooms. She connected with the children. She knew how frustrating it could be when people didn't understand her autism. Julia showed her students that they could be proud of who they were.

Julia wanted to keep helping other autistic people. There were a lot of organizations that did this, but Julia saw a problem with them. Many didn't have a single autistic person working there. *How can these organizations decide what's best for our community if they're not talking to anyone like me*? Julia wondered.

So Julia started working for a different kind of organization. The Autistic Self Advocacy Network (ASAN) is run by autistic people for autistic people. As the executive director, Julia makes sure there's room for all kinds of voices. She hires people from diverse backgrounds so they can share their ideas. When Julia speaks out about important issues, she draws on those hours she spent pacing and putting sentences together in her yard. Armed with her words, she celebrates everyone's unique brain and fights for their rights.

BORN MARCH 5, 1992
UNITED STATES OF AMERICA

"WE ARE FIGHTING FOR EVERYONE'S RIGHT TO SPEAK FOR THEMSELVES. WE ALL HAVE A VOICE, NO MATTER HOW WE EXPRESS IT, AND WE ARE ALL GOING TO BE HEARD."
—JULIA BASCOM

ILLUSTRATION BY TAYLOR BARRON

KEISHA CASTLE-HUGHES

ACTOR

SCAN TO HEAR MORE!

Once upon a time, there lived an imaginative girl named Keisha. She spent her days playing pretend, hanging out with her friends, and arguing with her brothers over whose turn it was to wash the dishes. Keisha had an ordinary childhood until a special person visited her school: a casting director.

The casting director was looking for a little girl to play the lead in a movie called *Whale Rider*. She had seen more than 10,000 girls for the role. None of them were quite right. But when she saw Keisha, she knew she'd found the movie's star. In no time, Keisha was transported to a land filled with lights and cameras.

Keisha played Pai, a determined Māori girl fighting to be the leader of her tribe. As people watched her sail across bright blue seas and swim with whales, they felt like they knew her. Keisha's performance was so strong she became the youngest person ever to earn an Oscar nomination for Best Actress.

After *Whale Rider*, Keisha continued to act. She made a lot of friends along the way. In 2014, something terrible happened. Her friend Charlotte died suddenly. Keisha was devastated. Charlotte had struggled with depression, and her friend's death inspired Keisha to talk about her own experience with bipolar disorder. She knew that bipolar, like depression, could make it harder to deal with life's ups and downs. If she spoke up, maybe others would realize they weren't alone.

So Keisha posted a message online, starting with the words: "My name is Keisha Castle-Hughes, and I am proud to tell you that I have bipolar disorder. Let's talk about it!" Soon, thousands of fans were responding, showing their support and love. Keisha wants everyone to understand that it's okay to feel sad sometimes, and that by talking about mental health, we can make the world a safer place.

BORN MARCH 24, 1990
AUSTRALIA AND NEW ZEALAND

"IT IS OUR DUTY TO TAKE THE TIME
TO ASK PEOPLE, CLOSE OR
STRANGER, WHO THEY ARE."
—KEISHA CASTLE-HUGHES

ILLUSTRATION BY
KATIE CRUMPTON

LISA LING

JOURNALIST

Lisa walked into the doctor's office as the camera followed her. She was used to being on camera, but normally, she was reporting on something else—a war in a foreign country, the lives of identical twins, or Indigenous people living on reservations. That day, she was reporting on herself.

By now, Lisa had been a journalist for many years. She had her own show that covered important issues affecting Americans. In one episode, she talked about the growing number of kids being diagnosed with ADHD. And as she spoke to kids with ADHD and their parents, something felt familiar to her.

When Lisa was in school, she had trouble focusing. Her teachers were always calling her parents to tell them she wasn't paying attention. Sometimes she'd go through entire class periods and realize she hadn't picked up a single thing the teacher said. It made her nervous when it came time to take tests.

As Lisa grew up, she still found her thoughts pulled in a million different directions. Once she found a topic she was interested in, though, she could work on it for hours. Her laser focus made her an incredible journalist. But Lisa had questions about the way her brain worked.

So Lisa decided to put herself in the story. For her episode on ADHD, she arranged for a doctor to test her and see if he could diagnose her. On camera, he told her she had ADD, or attention deficit disorder. Lisa felt relieved because her experiences finally had a name. It was like fitting a missing puzzle piece into her life.

Lisa saw her diagnosis as an opportunity for growth and understanding. She embraced her ADD as part of who she is. Lisa keeps telling incredible stories, understanding herself a little better now.

BORN AUGUST 30, 1973
UNITED STATES OF AMERICA

"FOR WHATEVER REASON, I AM THE WAY I AM, AND I'VE TRIED REALLY HARD TO NOT LET IT INHIBIT THE THINGS THAT ARE IMPORTANT TO ME."
—LISA LING

ILLUSTRATION BY LALA STELLUNE

MADELINE STUART

MODEL

On a breezy morning in Brisbane, Australia, Madeline and her mom went to a fashion show. Madeline watched in awe as beautiful models walked down the runway wearing vibrant outfits and eye-catching makeup. She knew at once that she wanted to be up there too.

Madeline left that fashion show feeling energized and inspired. With her mom's help, she began to pursue her new dream of becoming a model. When pictures from her first photo shoot went viral, almost overnight, Madeline became the first professional model with both Down syndrome and autism.

Down syndrome is a condition where some people are born with an extra chromosome, one of the tiny building blocks inside every person. Chromosomes store information about the traits kids inherit from their parents, like hair color and eye color. When people have an extra one, like Madeline, they look and act differently from people with a typical number of chromosomes. In the fashion industry, most models have similar looks, and there isn't usually a lot of room for uniqueness. But Madeline was determined to show the world how beautiful differences are.

After her photoshoot, designers were clamoring to have Madeline wear their clothes. Suddenly, Madeline found herself on one of the biggest catwalks in the fashion industry at New York Fashion Week. Reporters, critics, and photographers sat in the audience while Madeline prepared to take the stage. Wearing a glamorous white gown and striking blue makeup, Madeline took a deep breath and confidently walked down the runway with cameras flashing all around her.

Madeline wants to ensure there is space for all kinds of models—and that those models are treated well. She walks in shows, designs her own clothes, and speaks up to make fashion a more welcoming place for everyone.

BORN NOVEMBER 13, 1996

AUSTRALIA

"THERE HAS NEVER BEEN A SECOND WHEN I THOUGHT I COULDN'T DO IT. I LOVE MODELING AND THAT ALONE MAKES ME WORK HARD TO OVERCOME ANY OBSTACLES THAT I'M FACED WITH."
—MADELINE STUART

ILLUSTRATION BY JESS ROSE

MAGGIE ADERIN-POCOCK

SPACE SCIENTIST AND SCIENCE COMMUNICATOR

Once upon a time, there lived a girl named Maggie who dreamed of reaching the stars. From a young age, she was curious about the mysteries of the universe. She would spend hours gazing at planets and constellations, wondering about the secrets they held.

Maggie had dyslexia, which made reading and writing difficult for her. She would sit in the back of the class, feeling discouraged. But her interest in science kept her going. Once, her science teacher asked a question, and nobody else around her gave an answer. Maggie looked around. *I know this*, she thought. The answer seemed so obvious—but what if she was wrong? Maggie took a risk. She raised her hand. She was right!

When Maggie started working as a science communicator, she knew it was the best job for her. She talked to the public about scientific discoveries, theories, and experiments. Each time she gave a presentation about the universe or talked to kids about how they could work in science, she felt like she was sharing the magic of the night sky she'd loved as a little girl.

One day, Maggie was asked to co-host a television show about space. She was honored. She never thought she would be standing in a studio with other famous astronomers, teaching the public about the wonders of the solar system.

Aside from hosting her TV show, Maggie also wrote several books about space. Having dyslexia made writing challenging, but she worked through the difficulties to tell her stories. Her words flowed off the page and transported her readers to all of the planets and stars. She used engaging language and colorful pictures to show others how fun learning about space can be.

Maggie still dreams of reaching the stars, but for now she's exploring them from right here on earth.

BORN MARCH 9, 1968
UNITED KINGDOM

"IT'S OK TO FEEL OUTLANDISH IN A SYSTEM THAT ISN'T BUILT FOR YOU. IT IS JUST A REMINDER THAT YOU'RE DESIGNED TO MAKE A NEW ONE."
—MAGGIE ADERIN-POCOCK

ILLUSTRATION BY JEMMA JAMIE SKIDMORE

ONYINYE UDOKPORO

AUTHOR, ENTREPRENEUR, AND EDUCATOR

In a cozy living room on a summer's day, Onyinye eagerly waited for her students to arrive. At 12 years old, she had already built a growing list of clients for her tutoring services. She loved to help others learn, and she had a knack for teaching.

Onyinye had trouble reading and writing because of her dyslexia. Instead of letting that hold her back, she turned it into her superpower. Being dyslexic made Onyinye think creatively about ways to teach new topics aside from just reading from a book or writing an essay. *There's got to be a better way to learn*, Onyinye thought.

So she created Enrich Learning. It was an online platform where kids could get extra support with their studies.

She made sure her website was as accessible as possible. She never assumed everyone could easily read or write, so she used videos, interactive lessons, and pictures to make learning easier. Her website also allowed students to study at their own pace. She knew how important this was, especially for students with disabilities. It could be hard to keep up in a traditional classroom where other students were learning faster.

It's common for dyslexic people to feel less confident—something Onyinye experienced firsthand. Even when her business was doing well, she sometimes felt like she didn't belong as the head of the company. *What if I'm not a real entrepreneur?* she found herself thinking. When she feels this way, Onyinye remembers how hard she works and how her company makes people's lives better. That helps remind her that she's a strong, successful businesswoman.

BORN AUGUST 5, 1998
UNITED KINGDOM

"I WAS BORN TO DO THIS.
WHEN I SAY THIS IS THE
HAPPIEST I HAVE BEEN,
I MEAN IT!"
—ONYINYE UDOKPORO

ILLUSTRATION BY
ELIZABETH MONTERO SANTA

PAIGE LAYLE

ACTIVIST AND INFLUENCER

When Paige was little, people always commented on the way she acted. *You're so mature for your age!* they would say, or *What a sensitive young girl you are.* In public, she would act the way people expected her to. But after pretending for so long, she would have a meltdown, panicking and crying alone in her room.

Paige often felt different from other kids and had a hard time making friends. Simple things like making eye contact or being touched would overwhelm her.

Why do I feel this way? Paige wondered. Nobody seemed to have an answer.

But when she was a teenager, she finally got one. Her therapist told her she was autistic, and suddenly everything made sense.

One day, Paige saw someone online making fun of autistic people. She was upset. There was so much people didn't understand about autism. She decided to respond with a video, which she posted online.

Soon, millions of people were listening to what she had to say. On her TikTok, Paige educates people about what it's like to grow up autistic, how a diagnosis can change your life, and how it feels when people assume she's neurotypical. She also talks about how when doctors first studied autism, they mostly looked at how it affected boys. That meant that girls like her often went undiagnosed because their symptoms are different. Paige was asked to be on talk shows, give magazine interviews, and even voice a character in an audiobook.

Paige's millions of fans appreciate her for who she is—and Paige appreciates finally being able to be herself.

BORN AUGUST 2, 2000
CANADA

"IT MAKES ME SO HAPPY TO THINK THAT I'M HELPING PEOPLE."
—PAIGE LAYLE

ILLUSTRATION BY JOANNE DERTILI

POLETH MENDES

SHOT PUTTER

As Poleth stepped up to the throwing circle, she took a deep breath and focused on her goal. Her training and determination had gotten her this far. Now all she had to do was make her throw. With a mighty heave, she sent the ball flying through the air, farther than she'd ever thrown before. Poleth couldn't help but smile as she realized her dreams were coming true: she was about to become a gold medal Paralympian!

Poleth and her younger sister, Anaís, spent a lot of time training and playing games. Their childhood was filled with laughter, love, and friendly competition that pushed them to be their best.

Their favorite sport to play was called shot put. In shot put, athletes throw a heavy ball called a shot as far as they can, and the farthest throw wins. To be successful, you need a combination of extreme strength and precise aim. Poleth and Anaís lifted heavy weights, did deep squats, and hurled countless practice throws. Finally, they qualified for the Paralympics! They both competed in the F20 class, which is for athletes whose brains work differently than typical.

Not only did Poleth win the gold medal, but there was also a familiar face on the podium with her. Her sister Anaís had won bronze! It's rare for members of the same family to win medals at the same event. The women stood side by side, proudly receiving medals for Ecuador.

Before Poleth's triumphant victory, no athlete from Ecuador had ever won a medal in the Paralympics—but Poleth and Anaís won two! Everyone back home was thrilled. With Anaís at her side, Poleth achieved her dreams, and she couldn't wait to start training for her next big win.

BORN FEBRUARY 4, 1996

ECUADOR

Ecuador

ILLUSTRATION BY
PALOMA O'TOOLE

SALMA HAYEK

ACTOR

Once upon a time, there was a little girl with a big sense of humor. Salma loved playing pranks on her classmates. In the dorms at her boarding school in Louisiana, she would secretly change the alarm clocks, causing her friends to wake up way too early in the morning. Salma would laugh from her bed as the girls around her grumbled in confusion.

Between pranks, Salma went to class. She was a fast learner and did well in school. Although reading and writing took longer because of her dyslexia, she always felt that taking her time helped her understand things better.

After school, Salma went back to Mexico, where she'd grown up. There, she had a great opportunity. She starred in a local production of *Aladdin* and fell in love with acting. When she got older, she acted in TV shows in Mexico, and soon she was famous. Next stop: Hollywood!

Going to Hollywood was a big change. While Salma was a talented actor, she had a hard time getting cast. She didn't know English well, and there weren't a lot of Spanish-speaking roles in the United States. Casting directors would tell Salma she didn't have a future there. Salma decided to prove them wrong. She started to take English classes.

At first, she thought learning the language would be impossible, especially with her dyslexia. But she kept trying, taking all the time she needed to get things right.

Salma's hard work paid off, and it wasn't long before she started getting cast in movies. For Salma, it wasn't enough to be a famous actor. She wanted more opportunities for other Latinx actors. As a director and producer, she knows those casting directors she spoke to years ago were wrong. There's a future for her in Hollywood, and there's a future for Latinx women like her too.

BORN SEPTEMBER 2, 1966
MEXICO AND UNITED STATES OF AMERICA

"I'M VERY LUCKY I DIDN'T HAVE IT EASY, BECAUSE I'VE LEARNED SO MUCH FROM HAVING TO FIGURE OUT EVERYTHING ON MY OWN AND CREATE THINGS FOR MYSELF."
—SALMA HAYEK

ILLUSTRATION BY CHLOE FRIEDLEIN

SARAI PAHLA

DOCTOR AND MEDICAL TRANSLATOR

SCAN TO HEAR MORE!

Growing up in Zimbabwe, Sarai was always curious. She wanted to know everything from the lyrics of her favorite nursery rhymes to the reason behind the blue sky.

Sarai kept asking questions and learning the answers. Eventually, she became a doctor.

In Sarai's hospital in South Africa, there weren't enough doctors, and there wasn't enough money for medicine and equipment. Every day, she would come into work and hear the whirring of old machines and the sound of calls being made. She would see the large number of patients who needed her help. Without the necessary tools, Sarai couldn't do everything she wanted for those patients, and that made her sad.

Sarai decided to find another way to use her knowledge: medical translation. Being fluent in four languages, Sarai could help patients communicate with doctors who spoke different languages. She moved to Germany and started her own medical translation business.

While Sarai always knew she was a fast learner, she didn't understand why she was able to focus on such complex topics for so long. She also didn't understand why her social interactions were so different from what others expected, or why it was harder for her to have relationships. But in Germany, Sarai finally learned why. She is autistic. That led her to one more question: Why had it taken her so long to get an answer?

Sarai wasn't alone. Many autistic women don't get diagnosed until they are adults. Sarai wants to ensure that other young girls don't go as long as she did without an explanation for what makes them special.

BIRTHDATE UNKNOWN
ZIMBABWE, SOUTH AFRICA, AND GERMANY

"I TRY TO USE MY ABILITIES AND MY WEIRDNESS TO MAKE LIFE BETTER FOR THE OTHER PERSON."
—SARAI PAHLA

ILLUSTRATION BY
CARLA JAYE

SERINA HASEGAWA

SINGER

Serina squinted as her eyes adjusted to the bright lights on the stage. The audience waited eagerly for the music to begin. She stood proudly beside her bandmates, the talented members of Little Glee Monster, an all-girl pop band from Japan.

As the music started, Serina felt a burst of energy. Her powerful voice echoed through the venue, enchanting everyone who listened. It wove into beautiful harmonies as all the band members sang the catchy tune. The girls bounced to the beat, dancing through multicolored stage lights. It was an amazing show and a great way to start their first tour.

Between shows, Serina practiced dance moves and high notes with the rest of the band. But she was also dealing with bipolar disorder and attention deficit hyperactivity disorder (ADHD).

Serina poured her heart into her music and shared her love with her fans. It was not always easy, but therapy and medication helped. Support from her bandmates did too. She worked hard to manage her mental health and continue shining on stage.

However, in 2022, Serina made the difficult decision to leave Little Glee Monster to focus on her health. She knew that taking care of herself was important, and it was time to take a break. One day, she hoped, she'd return to those bright stage lights.

Her bandmates and fans supported her every step of the way. As Serina continues her journey toward healing, she gives hope to fans who find strength in her experiences. She shows them that even when life feels difficult, there's always a reason to keep moving forward.

BORN JUNE 1, 1998
JAPAN

"ISN'T IT IMPORTANT TO BE YOURSELF AT ALL TIMES? NO HIDING, NO SHAME."
—SERINA HASEGAWA

ILLUSTRATION BY DONG QIU

SIENA CASTELLON

AUTHOR AND ADVOCATE

In a small Irish town nestled between lush hills, there lived an extraordinary girl named Siena who loved to help people. When she saw a problem, she immediately wanted to fix it. One day, while navigating the vast world of the internet, 13-year-old Siena became frustrated. She realized that most online resources about children with special educational needs (SEN) were aimed at parents, not the children themselves. Siena was autistic and had dyslexia, ADHD, and dyspraxia, which meant she had trouble with motor skills like tying her shoes. Where were the resources for students like her?

I could change this, Siena thought. She set out to create a website for SEN students. Siena's site was filled with guidance, support, and encouragement for neurodivergent kids. It gave SEN students the tools they needed to learn.

Her website was a huge success, and Siena knew she could offer even more. She wrote a book called *The Spectrum Girl's Survival Guide: How to Grow Up Awesome and Autistic*. She wanted girls like her to have help dealing with situations she'd found confusing, like reading body language, expressing themselves, and understanding their own emotions. And who better to give advice than someone who understood what they were going through?

But Siena still had more to do. In 2018, she created Neurodiversity Celebration Week (NCW), an event that teaches others about neurological disorders. Thousands of people showed up, excited to share their neurodivergent pride. They dived into the online workshops, panels, and activities Siena planned. She wanted them all to understand that neurodiversity isn't something to be afraid of or embarrassed about—it's something to celebrate.

Siena keeps using her problem-solving skills to help people. She proves that sometimes the right solution requires thinking differently.

BORN AUGUST 2, 2000
IRELAND AND UNITED KINGDOM

"I BELIEVE THAT SOMETIMES THE THINGS WE FIND THE HARDEST AND THE MOST CHALLENGING ARE THE THINGS THAT ARE MOST WORTH DOING."
—SIENA CASTELLON

ILLUSTRATION BY
ZUZA KAMIŃSKA

SUSAN TE KAHURANGI KING

ARTIST

In a land of enchanting colors, there lived a talented artist named Susan. Susan was a quiet soul who expressed herself through the language of art. Though she stopped speaking when she was young, her vibrant drawings spoke volumes, telling magical stories without words.

Susan's artistic journey began when she was a little girl. She used pencils and crayons to create fascinating characters and whimsical worlds. Her autism allowed her to see the world in a different light, and her drawings were filled with fantastical creatures, swirling colors, and mesmerizing patterns that seemed to dance off the page. She didn't make sketches or plan things out, but she also never used an eraser.

As Susan grew older, her artwork grew more intricate and detailed. Some people didn't understand Susan or the way she worked. *This looks so different from any art we've seen*, they would say. But for others, Susan's unusual style was refreshing. People from far and wide have come to marvel at Susan's masterpieces. They admire the bold lines and eye-catching textures that adorn the paper. The longer people look at Susan's drawings, the more they can discover in them. Her art has hung in galleries and museums, making people stop and take notice when they pass by.

For some time, Susan felt sad and uninspired, and she stopped drawing. This pause went on for many years. In her own time, and thanks to her family's encouragement, Susan did pick up her pen again and let the ink blossom across her paper, beginning a new masterpiece.

Susan is still creating today. Her work inspires others to embrace their own unique voices—regardless of whether they can be heard out loud.

BORN 1951

NEW ZEALAND

ILLUSTRATION BY
AKIRASERENE

TEMPLE GRANDIN

PROFESSOR OF ANIMAL SCIENCES

SCAN TO HEAR MORE!

Once there was a girl named Temple from Boston, who was often described as different. With a unique and brilliant mind, Temple was inquisitive and loved to learn. But people didn't always understand the way she behaved. As a child, doctors said she had "brain damage." That wasn't right, though. Temple was autistic and would grow up to be a talented author and educator.

Temple didn't speak until she was three years old. But from an early age, she had a deep love and understanding for animals, especially cows. As she grew up, she believed she could see the world through their eyes and feel what they felt. This incredible connection inspired her to become an animal behaviorist, someone who studies how animals think and behave.

"Autism helped me understand animals because I think in pictures," Temple said. "Since animals do not have language, their memories have to be sensory-based instead of word-based."

Temple saw that animals were not always happy on farms. She could tell when they were scared or stressed, so she designed herding equipment and special enclosures to help them feel more comfortable. Because of her work, many farmers understood their animals better. It made them think in ways they never had before.

Temple's work also helped people understand autism and the gifts that come with it. Two of her most famous books are *Thinking in Pictures* and *Animals in Translation*. In these books, Temple shared the way autism impacted her and her work.

Thanks to Temple's tireless work as an activist and educator, the world knows more about what it means to think differently.

BORN AUGUST 29, 1947
UNITED STATES OF AMERICA

"THE MOST IMPORTANT THING PEOPLE DID FOR ME WAS TO EXPOSE ME TO NEW THINGS."
—TEMPLE GRANDIN

ILLUSTRATION BY
BEATRICE CEROCCHI

KEEP THINKING CREATIVELY

TELL YOUR TALE

It's time to explore the Rebel you know the best—you! All you need is a piece of paper, something to write and draw with, and your imagination.

1. Fold a piece of paper in half on the long end, like a book, then unfold it.

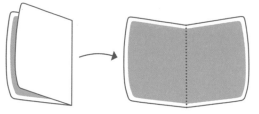

2. Think about how you want to tell your story. What would you want readers to know about you if you were featured in a Rebel Girls book?

3. On the left side of the fold, write your name in big bright letters. Then, write your story.

STORYTELLING TIPS

There are lots of ways to tell your story.

- You can start with "Once upon a time . . ." like in Salma Hayek's story or jump right into the action like in Chamique Holdsclaw's.
- Consider telling a story about when you were little or sharing a moment when you were extra proud of yourself.
- Make sure to add lots of details.
- If you are describing a moment in your life, close your eyes and remember what that moment was like. Then describe what it looked like, how it smelled, and the sounds you heard.

DRAW YOUR PORTRAIT

Channel your inner artist and make a self-portrait, or picture of yourself.

1. What materials would you like to use? Colored pencils? Crayons? Pens? Watercolors? Do you like to draw or paint? Gather your supplies.

2. On the right side of the fold, draw your portrait.

UNIQUE YOU

Every self-portrait is different. What do you want your picture to show?

- You can show yourself posing like Onyinye Udokporo or doing an activity like Daria Saville.
- You can focus on your face or show yourself from your head to your feet — or anything in between.
- The portrait can be realistic or abstract, colorful or black and white — however you see yourself.
- Don't forget the background! It can also be realistic or abstract. What does the background of your portrait share about you?

3. When you're done, you can share your story and portrait with a friend or family member, hang it up, or even keep it tucked inside this book.

DANCE YOUR HEART OUT

Serina Hasegawa sang and danced onstage with Little Glee Monster. But you don't have to be a professional performer to enjoy dancing. Not only is it fun, it's also a great way to switch things up and get moving if you've been sitting and focusing for a long time. You can dance by yourself or ask a friend or family member to join you.

1. Pick out a song or a playlist that makes you want to move. If you're not sure where to start, check out some of Little Glee Monster's songs.
2. Start off by getting comfortable and moving to the music. Listen to the beat, pick out your favorite instrument, or pay attention to the lyrics and see how your body responds.
3. Once you feel warmed up, you can make up your own choreography—patterns of steps and movements that go along with the music.
4. If you're dancing with someone else, take turns adding one move at a time until you have a whole dance routine.

TELL A STORY WITH PICTURES

Video journalist Fahima Abdulrahman and artist Susan Te Kahurangi King both use images to tell stories and express themselves. Try it out and see how creative you can be.

1. Think of something that happened to you recently that you might want to tell someone about. It could be a funny story or a surprising experience you had.
2. Think about how you could explain what happened without using words. What pictures would you show?
3. Once you have some images in mind, you can try:
    - Creating a comic strip without words
    - Filming a video
    - Taking photos and organizing them into an album on a phone
    - Making a collage using images from the internet or a magazine

EXPLORE THE NIGHT SKY

Science communicator Maggie Aderin-Pocock helps people see the magic of the stars. She uses a high-powered telescope to see into space, but you can explore parts of the universe without one.

1. With the help of an adult, go online and look up what you might be able to see in the night sky. Be sure to find information about the area where you live and the time of year, since the stars and planets look different depending on where you are and when you're stargazing.
2. You can look for guides on how to find specific stars or planets, or how to spot constellations. Constellations are groups of stars that astronomers decided look like figures from mythology.
3. On a clear night, ask your grown-up for permission to go outside and look up at the stars. See if you can spot any of the things you read about.
4. Make up your own constellations. What do the different clusters of stars remind you of? Do you see any pictures or patterns?
5. If you're looking at the stars with a friend or family member, describe the constellation you made up and see if the other person can spot it.

SORT IT OUT

Did you notice how the women in this book are organized? We put them in alphabetical order by first name, from Amanda Gorman to Temple Grandin, but there are a lot of other ways you could sort them. Choose a different method—here are some ideas:

- By birthdate from youngest to oldest
- By the country they come from
- By the background color of their illustration

Once you have a sequence you like, write it down. Try reading the book in that order next time and see if it changes your experience!

ABOUT THE AUTHOR

Shadae B. Mallory, MA, is a writer, educator, and social justice advocate. Shadae earned their Bachelor of Arts in English from the University of Northern Colorado (2017) and their Master of Arts in College Student Personnel from Bowling Green State University (2019). They live in northern Colorado where they spend most of their time with their partner, dogs, chickens, and pet catfish, Daryl. You can follow them online at ShadaeMallory.com.

LISTEN TO MORE EMPOWERING STORIES ON THE REBEL GIRLS APP!

Download the app to listen to beloved Rebel Girls stories, as well as brand-new tales of extraordinary women. Filled with the adventures and accomplishments of women from around the world and throughout history, the Rebel Girls app is designed to entertain, inspire, and build confidence in listeners everywhere.

THE ILLUSTRATORS

Twenty extraordinary female and nonbinary artists from all over the world illustrated the portraits in this book.

AKIRASERENE, **USA**, 53

BEATRICE CEROCCHI, **ITALY**, 55

CARLA JAYE, **UK**, 11, 47

CHARLOTTE GRANGE, **UK**, 17

CHLOE FRIEDLEIN, **USA**, 45

DONG QIU, **CHINA**, 19, 49

ELIZABETH MONTERO SANTA,
  DOMINICAN REPUBLIC, 21, 39

ERICA ROOT, **USA**, 25

JEMMA JAMIE SKIDMORE, **UK**, 37

JESS ROSE, **UK**, 35

JOANNE DERTILI, **GREECE**, 41

KATIE CRUMPTON, **USA**, 15, 31

KETURAH ARIEL, **USA**, 7

LALA STELLUNE, **INDONESIA**, 27, 33

PALOMA O'TOOLE, **SPAIN**, 43

PAU ZAMRO, **MEXICO**, 23

PAULA ZORITE, **SPAIN**, 9

TAYLOR BARRON, **USA**, 29

VERONICA GUARINO, **THAILAND**, 13

ZUZA KAMIŃSKA, **POLAND**, 51

MORE BOOKS!

For more stories about amazing women and girls, check out other Rebel Girls books.

ABOUT REBEL GIRLS

REBEL GIRLS, a certified B Corporation, is a global, multi-platform empowerment brand dedicated to helping raise the most inspired and confident generation of girls through content, experiences, products, and community. Originating from an international best-selling children's book, Rebel Girls amplifies stories of real-life, extraordinary women throughout history, geography, and field of excellence. With a growing community of 30 million self-identified Rebel Girls spanning more than 100 countries, the brand engages with Generation Alpha through its book series, premier app and audio content, events, and merchandise. To date, Rebel Girls has sold more than 11 million books in 50 languages and reached 40 million audio listens. Award recognition includes *New York Times* bestseller list, 2022 Apple Design Award for Social Impact, multiple Webby Awards for family & kids and education, and Common Sense Media Selection honors among many others.

As a B Corp, we're part of a global community of businesses that meet high standards of social and environmental impact.

Join the Rebel Girls community:

    Facebook: facebook.com/rebelgirls
    Instagram: @rebelgirls
    X/Twitter: @rebelgirlsbook
    TikTok: @rebelgirlsbook
    App: rebelgirls.com/audio
    Podcast: rebelgirls.com/podcast
    Web: rebelgirls.com

If you liked this book, please take a moment to review it wherever you prefer!